THE CONDITIONS
OF SUCCESS

THIS IS THE TWENTY-FIRST OF THE
WALTER NEURATH MEMORIAL LECTURES
WHICH ARE GIVEN ANNUALLY EACH SPRING ON
SUBJECTS REFLECTING THE INTERESTS OF
THE FOUNDER
OF THAMES AND HUDSON

THE DIRECTORS WISH TO EXPRESS
PARTICULAR GRATITUDE TO THE GOVERNORS AND
MASTER OF BIRKBECK COLLEGE
UNIVERSITY OF LONDON
FOR THEIR GRACIOUS SPONSORSHIP OF
THESE LECTURES

THE CONDITIONS
OF SUCCESS

HOW THE MODERN ARTIST
RISES TO FAME

ALAN BOWNESS

THAMES AND HUDSON

Printed and bound in Great Britain by Balding and Mansell Ltd, Wisbech

The text that follows is that of the lecture given on 7 March 1989 at the University of London, with very little alteration. The lecture itself was given without illustration, so that the audience could concentrate on the argument – the matter being speculative and provocative, rather than art historical. I would like to thank the Master of Birkbeck College, Tessa Blackstone, for hosting the lecture, and the Neurath Family – Eva, Thomas and Constance – for their invitation. Their achievement in continuing to run the firm of Thames and Hudson so successfully now seems to me to match that of its founder, Walter Neurath, in whose name these lectures are given.

1 The author with Alison Smithson at the *54:64* exhibition at the Tate Gallery in April 1964. The painting behind them is Michael Andrews's *All Night Long*, 1963–64.

THERE IS A GENERAL SUPPOSITION even among the educated public that there is something arbitrary about artistic success. Stories about genius dying unrecognized, or artists starving in garrets, are common enough. The public perception of the way in which the artist rises to fame is coloured by such myths. Even if it is accepted that they are untrue, or at least exaggerated, people are reluctant to believe that chance does not generally play a major role in the rising fortunes of an artist.

I want to propose a contrary position, and argue that there is a clear and regular progression towards artistic success. There are, in my view, conditions of success, which can be exactly described. And success is conditioned, in an almost deterministic way. Artistic fame is predictable.

I have given this essay a subtitle, 'How the Modern Artist Rises to Fame', and first I must define my terms. It seems to me that the idea of the modern artist – and this includes writers and musicians – emerges with the Romantic movement: more explicitly perhaps that it goes back to what the Germans call the *Geniebewegung* (genius movement) of the later eighteenth century. There does seem to be a real change in the status of the creative artist at that point, and in certain respects nothing essential has altered since.

Any number of significant events can be adduced to mark this change: what is common is the new sense of independence or, better, freedom, that the artist possesses. Although there are certain precedents in seventeenth-century Holland, it was the appearance of a powerful middle class in eighteenth-century England that gave

2 Turner's watercolour *Transept of Ewenny Priory, Glamorganshire* was among the works shown at the 1797 Royal Academy Summer Exhibition when the twenty-two-year-old painter's outstanding talents were first recognized.

new opportunities to artists. One of the first to seize them was Turner, securely independent after his first Academy success in 1797 at the age of twenty-two and his election as member of the Royal Academy four years later. Turner is in many respects the paradigm of the modern artist with whom I am concerned.

Turner is a very special kind of artist, and before proceeding further I have to make a distinction, crude and not absolute, but nevertheless essential for the argument, between the artist as genius and the artist as journeyman, and between art for the museums and art for the market. The two divisions are related – it is the journeymen who supply the market, and the masters – the artists of genius – whose work, hopefully, fills the museums.

The art market expanded enormously in the nineteenth century. In the first half it was the more or less annual exhibitions of the Paris Salon and the London Royal Academy that were dominant: in 1850 3,923 works were exhibited in Paris and 1,456 in London. Several thousand artists were involved. Such exhibitions attracted enormous attendances: there were references to the salons having a million visitors, that is, approximately the same figure as the population of Paris. In the second half of the nineteenth century we have the rise of the independent societies, and then of the private dealers, and the market grows still more. The pattern continues into the twentieth century, with the public museums and art galleries also playing their part. But nothing significant changes.

The art market has sustained an enormous volume of activity, and now absorbs the production of hundreds of artists. The vast majority of them are what I have called journeymen – they have served an apprenticeship, and can produce honest, decent work, which is the art that most people want. They are not, however, the masters, the artists of genius, who have an extraordinary capacity for imaginative creation and original thought. Inevitably, artists of genius are few in number. You will not find many of them showing

3 Van Gogh's *Irises* of 1889 became the world's most expensive painting when sold at Sotheby's, New York, on 11 December 1987 for $53.9 million (approximately £30 million).

their work in the annual exhibitions of the Royal Academy, either today or 150 years ago. On the other hand, the museum collection aspires to show a chronological sequence of the work of such artists, carrying forward an argument which forms the material of any history of modern art.

It is these exceptional artists on whom I now want to concentrate, asking the question how they achieve recognition. But before I continue I want to make one point. At the early stages of their careers the market is largely indifferent to the work of such artists, then at a certain moment this situation changes dramatically. It is only the museum artists whose work begins to rise to exceptional prices, and of course it is the very rarity of such artists in a supply-and-demand market that accounts for the phenomenal prices achieved today in the auction houses. If the work of art happens to be a painting or sculpture, rather than a poem or a musical composition, it is a unique object, and this permits the extraordinary exploitation of a market that attempts to convince us that Van Gogh's *Irises* painting is actually worth £30 million.

As it happens, Van Gogh is, like Turner, another good example to illustrate my thesis of the inevitability of artistic success, though it may appear at first that he proves the opposite.

THERE ARE FOUR SUCCESSIVE CIRCLES of recognition through which the exceptional artist passes on his path to fame. I will call them peer recognition, critical recognition, patronage by dealers and collectors, and finally public acclaim.

Peer recognition is the first and in many ways the most significant. By peers I mean the young artist's equals, his exact artist contemporaries, and then the wider circle of practising artists. In general, they can be highly perceptive, though they may occasionally be obtuse and sometimes jealous of a younger artist's success.

In any group of artists, some stand out. You can see this happening among art students, and it is sometimes at first a matter of personality as much as it is of achievement. And of course the emergence of exceptional talent is not a phenomenon confined to the world of art: it happens in every field.

Let me illustrate this point with a personal anecdote. Early in 1960 Lawrence Gowing and I were buying paintings for the Arts Council collection. We thought that it would be an encouraging gesture if we purchased something from the annual exhibition of the London Group – a long established artists' society, with a distinguished history. Lawrence and I walked round and round the exhibition looking for something to buy. This was a somewhat dispiriting experience, and the paintings by artists whose work we knew was not always their best. Eventually we settled on *November*, an impressive abstract painting, rather in the manner of Alan Davie, by someone of whom neither Lawrence nor I had ever heard, and recommended that the Arts Council should buy it.

They did, but pointed out to us that we were buying the work of a twenty-two-year-old student in his first year at the Royal College of Art, and thus could scarcely be said to be encouraging the generally middle-aged members of the London Group. Our supportive gesture had misfired.

The point of the story, however, is that the unknown painter was David Hockney. In other words, it was quite obvious to a forty-year-old painter/teacher like Gowing and to a thirty-year-old art historian/art critic like myself that here was an exceptional talent. I went to see Hockney in the Painting School of the Royal College – this was early in 1960 – and met some other painters in his year – R.B. Kitaj, Allen Jones, Peter Phillips, Derek Boshier – about as remarkable a group as any art school has ever gathered together. They were bent upon developing a new kind of painting in reaction to the American-influenced abstraction that had swept through the

4 David Hockney's *November*, 1959, shown at the 1960 London Group exhibition.

5 David Hockney's *We Two Boys Together Clinging*, painted when Hockney was a student at the Royal College of Art, and acquired in 1961 by the Arts Council.

6 *(opposite, above)* R.B. Kitaj's *The Red Banquet*, painted in 1960 when Kitaj was a student at the Royal College of Art, and a prize-winning painting at the 1961 John Moores Exhibition, Liverpool.

7 *(opposite, below)* Allen Jones's *The Battle of Hastings*, painted in 1961–62 when the artist was undertaking a one-year teacher's training course at Hornsey College of Art after being asked to leave the Royal College of Art. It was purchased soon after completion by the collector E.J. Power.

British art colleges in the late 1950s. In their first year these painters were not popular with the College authorities – indeed, Allen Jones was asked to leave – but by the end of the three-year course everyone was convinced. David won the Gold Medal, and received it in golden jacket and with golden hair. His own work had changed in character, and in 1961 he had allowed the Arts Council to exchange the immature abstract painting for a new one, *We Two Boys Together Clinging*, now recognized as one of his first masterpieces. Two years later, in 1963, the Tate Gallery acquired its first Hockney, *The First Marriage* (1962).

The gathering together of a group of talented painters, as happened at the Royal College in London in 1959–60, is significant in itself, and I will return to this question later when I discuss the psychology of artistic creativity. It is striking how often new beginnings in modern art arise out of such early conjunctions of outstanding talents. Think of the Pre-Raphaelites, or of Monet, Renoir, Sisley and Bazille meeting in the Parisian studio of Gabriel-Charles Gleyre in 1862, or Kirchner, Schmidt-Rottluff and Heckel in Dresden in 1906 – in every case, a group of painters still in their early twenties.

At this stage in my argument, the point that I want to make is that it is always the artists themselves who are first to recognize exceptional talent. This is true even with such difficult painters as Van Gogh. He had the misfortune of starting in the wrong place, and this is again something I want to discuss later, when I talk about relocation and dislocation, factors that can play a consider-able part in the artist's path to success. But when in February 1886 Van Gogh arrived in Paris for the two-year stay during which he was to totally transform his art it is striking that he quickly met all the outstanding talents of the new Post-Impressionist generation – Gauguin and Bernard, Signac and Seurat. I do not believe they would have bothered with this difficult and uncouth Dutchman

8–10 The young Pre-Raphaelites: Dante Gabriel Rossetti's self-portrait aged twenty-seven *(above left)*; Holman Hunt's portrait of John Everett Millais aged twenty-three *(above right)* and Holman Hunt's self-portrait aged eighteen *(right)*.

11 Fantin-Latour's *L'Atelier des Batignolles*: a homage to Manet, who is shown painting, watched by younger fellow artists – Renoir, Monet,

Bazille – and admiring critics – Astruc, Maître and Zola. It was exhibited at the 1870 Paris Salon.

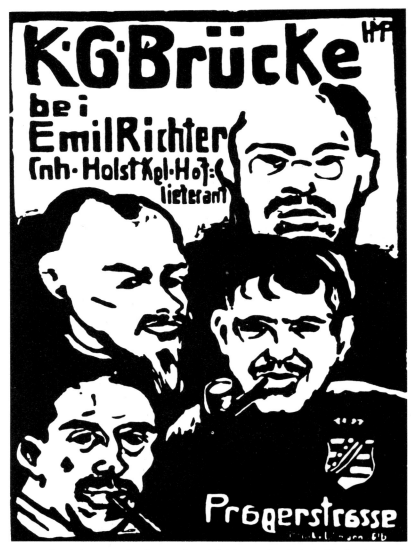

12 Pechstein's poster for the *Brücke* exhibition at the Galerie Emil Richter, in Dresden, in 1909, with portraits of Heckel and Schmidt-Rottluff (top left and right) and of Pechstein and Kirchner (bottom left and right). The artists were all still in their twenties.

had they not believed that in him an extraordinary new kind of painting was struggling to be born.

Older artists can be jealous and suspicious, as was Cézanne, who thought Gauguin had stolen his 'petite sensation'. A few seem by nature to be generous-minded, as was Pissarro, who recognized and encouraged Cézanne and Gauguin and Seurat and Van Gogh, all at a remarkably early stage in their careers. Maybe this generosity of spirit is why, in the last resort, Pissarro is not their equal.

IF THE FIRST STAGE OF RECOGNITION comes from the artistic community, the second stage comes from those who write and talk about art – the critics. (And I mean serious critics, and not art journalists.) It is true that the critics' role is parasitic, but the artist cannot do without them: they are not to artists what ornithologists are to birds, as has been claimed.

The writer on art has two important functions: the first is to help create the verbal language that allows us to talk about art. Painting and sculpture are, like music, non-verbal arts, but it is impossible to discuss them without recourse to words. In the case of music, Hans Keller tried to develop a musical analysis of music with some success among the musically literate, but no one has pursued the visual analysis of the visual arts, so far as I know. Thus we are forced into the creation of a new vocabulary to discuss any new art.

Some artists can do this themselves without difficulty. Indeed, most artists write well, perhaps because they naturally seek out concrete and precise terms, as befits the object maker. But when they have to put their ideas in words and defend their artistic position many turn to their writer friends.

One of the most personal and eloquent statements made by a sculptor is the short text, *The Sculptor's Aims*, which Henry Moore contributed to *Unit One* in 1934. It is almost too eloquent, and not entirely characteristic of Moore's other writings. Knowing that

13   Manet's portrait of Zola, painted in 1867–68 when the painter was thirty-five and the novelist twenty-seven. Zola had written enthusiastically about Manet's work in 1866 and Manet painted this portrait out of gratitude and gave it to the young critic. Zola's widow gave it to the Louvre.

Herbert Read was editor of *Unit One*, I once asked Read if he had had a hand in writing it. He smiled and wanted to know why I had asked the question. I told him that I had observed a painter friend describing his work in the words that I had used in writing of his art. Read agreed that this happened all the time: yes, he and Moore had written *The Sculptor's Aims* together.

For the writer, the challenge of inventing a language to describe new art is an exciting and worthwhile one. He is appealing to a broader audience for an understanding of something in which he personally believes. This kind of art critic tends to write about the artists who are a little older than he is: he can see very clearly that the artist he is championing is outstanding in his generation, and very often he writes, as it were, out of the artistic community. An excellent example of this phenomenon is the young Émile Zola, whose articles in *L'Événement* on the Salon of 1866 included the famous and unprecedented prediction that 'M. Manet's place in the Louvre is marked out, like that of Courbet, like that of any artist of original and strong temperament'. Zola's language was his own, but his views were essentially those of his close friend from boyhood, Cézanne, and those of Cézanne's artist friends.

The fact that Zola did not go on to promote the exceptional talents of Cézanne has occasioned much comment, but does not surprise me. As we know from *L'Œuvre*, in Zola's view Cézanne was a failure, and after the publication of the novel in 1886 the two men never met again. I have some sympathy for Zola's position, for it is hard to accept that one has been at school with a genius. Zola and Cézanne knew one another too well.

I realized recently that my own experience confirms this situation. I was most active as a writer on new art in the late 1950s and early 1960s, when I wrote at length on Pasmore, Hepworth, William Scott, Davie, Hilton, Lanyon, Heron — all artists ten to twenty-five years older than myself. I was certainly very interested in

14 Courbet's portrait of Baudelaire, painted probably in 1848 when the painter was twenty-nine and the poet twenty-seven. The two young men had much in common, but Baudelaire never wrote in support of Courbet's art.

the work of my own exact contemporaries – Harold and Bernard Cohen, Denny, Richard Smith, Ayres, Riley, Tilson, Jack Smith, Hill, Kossoff and Auerbach, Hockney, Blake, Jones, Kitaj, Hodgkin – but I did not write at length about them, though I chose their work for exhibitions with which I was involved and recommended it for purchase by public and private bodies.

Perhaps this indicates a general rule: one can multiply examples of the narrowness of the writer promoting new art again and again. Baudelaire did not really get beyond Delacroix (twenty years older), and thought Guys (fifteen years older) was the painter of modern life, rather than his exact contemporary Courbet, who waited in vain for Baudelaire's support. Douglas Cooper championed the Cubists, half a generation older than he was, and not the abstract painters who were his contemporaries. It helps perhaps if you come late to modern art, as was the case with Herbert Read. He wrote authoritatively about Moore and Hepworth and Nicholson, who belonged to his generation. Or with Clement Greenberg, who in his *Horizon* article of 1948 could see with great clarity that Jackson Pollock and David Smith had lifted American painting and sculpture on to a new and higher plane. It is hard for us to appreciate the originality of such a statement: pity the writer on contemporary art, whose opinions to later generations seem ridiculous if wrong and commonplace if right.

This brings me to the second valuable role that the writer plays in the modern artist's rise to fame – his contribution to the critical debate. Judgments in art are not absolute or final: they are sustained by consensus. I began my university career as a student of F. R. Leavis at Downing College, Cambridge, and have always regarded Leavis as the ideal modern critic. The titles of his books tell us a great deal – *New Bearings*, in which the young Leavis sorts out the poets half a generation older than himself, and defends still-contested figures such as Eliot; *Revaluation*, in which he questions

15 *The Council of the Royal Academy Selecting Pictures for the Exhibition*, exhibited in 1876 and painted by Charles West Cope (1811–90). He was elected ARA at thirty-two, full

RA at thirty-six, and showed 134 paintings at Summer Exhibitions; he is not represented in the Tate Collection. The members of the Academy's Council are all practising artists.

established reputations; *The Great Tradition*, into which he placed a small hierarchy of nineteenth-century English novelists; *The Common Pursuit*, which was the critical debate in which we are all participating.

Despite his reputation for intolerance, Leavis was as a teacher surprisingly humble. He treated the freshest of students as a potential colleague who was now embarking on an ongoing discussion with the whole fraternity of literary critics. He reminded us that critical opinions carried an implied interrogative, as if the words, 'this is true, is it not?', stood at the end of every statement.

Once the critical consensus is established, changes are relatively minor. Reputations rise and fall, but within restricted limits. An artist's career is not completed until his death, and early work is constantly reviewed in the light of what the artist does later. Similarly, the ever-changing art of the present compels us to review the art of the past. But having said this, I do not believe that the

16 A photograph of the Paris Salon of 1852, showing the crowded conditions under which paintings were exhibited. Courbet's *Demoiselles de village faisant l'aumône à une gardeuse de vaches* is prominently shown on the left-hand wall, perhaps because it had just been purchased by the Prince-President's half-brother.

17 The poster for the Fifth Impressionist Exhibition held in April 1880: Renoir, Monet and Sisley were absent, as they had decided to show in the 1880 Salon. Unlike Degas, who could afford to stay independent, they desperately needed sales and could reasonably regard success in the official Salon as still the only way to achieve this.

general outlines of the history of art up to, say, twenty years ago, are now going to change very much.

The revival of interest in French Salon painting will, for example, deepen our understanding of Degas, but anyone who believes that Gérôme and Bouguereau are Degas' equals is talking nonsense. Similarly, those who today think that Modernism has somehow failed, and that we can now ignore it, are surely misguided. What has happened is that we are all now critical of any 'one straight line' theory of artistic progress, which has always been a superimposition on the general consensus by certain art critics or by the artists themselves.

Sorting out what has happened in the last twenty years is a further essential part of the critics' contribution to the artist's rise to fame. This is particularly clear if we consider the role of survey exhibitions of contemporary art, which are generally presented by the critic, albeit in the allied role of exhibition organizer or museum director. Exhibitions such as the second Post-Impressionist exhibition or the Cologne Sonderbund or the Armory Show, all held in the years immediately before the 1914–18 War, imposed a revolutionary view of recent art history that was later to win general acceptance.

I had the chance to do something of this kind in 1964 when with Lawrence Gowing and Philip James and the financial support of the Gulbenkian Foundation we made a very large exhibition of

18 A painting, ascribed to Roger Fry, of one of the galleries of the Second Post-Impressionist Exhibition, which opened in London in October 1912. Having presented Manet, Gauguin, Van Gogh and Cézanne in the 1910 exhibition, Fry now concentrated on promoting Matisse and Picasso.

19 One of the Van Gogh rooms at the Cologne Sonderbund Exhibition of 1912. Modelled on Fry's 1910 exhibition, the Sonderbund show gave overwhelming prominence to Van Gogh, with 125 works. The other featured artists were Cézanne (26 works), Gauguin (25 works), Cross (17 works), Signac (18 works) and Picasso (16 works).

contemporary art at the Tate Gallery. It was called *54:64 Painting and Sculpture of a Decade*, and we tried to establish a cohesive picture of what had been happening to modern art. The more significant artists of the decade were each represented by a group of five works, usually singled out with colour plates in the catalogue. Lesser (or younger) figures had one or two works only. Looking back after twenty-five years I can see that we omitted some major figures such as Richard Hamilton and Andy Warhol and that some promising talents have faded. But on the whole I would still defend our choice and claim that it helped establish the critical consensus of today. We were, for example, the first to show prominently the work of Jasper Johns in the United Kingdom – five major paintings by the artist I would now regard as America's finest.

In presenting such an exhibition the informed critic is not trying to impose his personal taste on the public. He is offering a responsible choice. By virtue of the fact that he has spent a great deal of time looking at the art of today, talking with the artists, reading his fellow critics, he acquires an authority which has to be recognized. It does not make him popular with artists, most of whom are bound to be deeply disappointed by the choices. After the 1964 exhibition I was happy to retreat from the turmoil of contemporary art into the safer world of French nineteenth-century painting where artists are dead and unable to argue back.

It was gratifying to find a younger triumvirate of Norman Rosenthal, Christos Joachimedes and Nicholas Serota coming forward at the Royal Academy in 1981 with a somewhat similarly intentioned exhibition, *A New Spirit in Painting*. Thirty-eight artists were chosen, most of them in their thirties or forties and coming more or less equally from the United States, Italy, Germany and the United Kingdom. There were only two French artists included, both from a much older generation. A view of contemporary art was proposed, which has, by and large, won a considerable measure of acceptance.

Such exhibitions are only the most prominent examples of the process of presenting new art to the public which goes on all the time. Museums of modern art play their part here. When he began to build up the collection of the Museum of Modern Art in New York in 1929, Alfred Barr was able to present a view of twentieth-century art and then watch a minority opinion win near universal approval. It is a matter of considerable regret that the advent of the Second World War prevented Herbert Read and Peggy Guggenheim from doing something similar in London.

Directors of national museums, such as the Tate Gallery, have less freedom of action. John Rothenstein championed Edward Burra, who won acceptance, and Roy de Maistre, who did not.

20 An installation view of the exhibition 54:64 *Painting and Sculpture of a Decade* at the Tate Gallery in 1964, designed by Alison and Peter Smithson. The photograph shows David Smith's *Cubi X*, two of Motherwell's *Elegies to the Spanish Republic*, and Kline's *Meryon*, later acquired by the Tate Gallery.

21 An installation view of the Francis Bacon retrospective exhibition at the Tate Gallery in May–August 1985, showing two late works: *Diptych*, 1982–84, and *Oedipus and the Sphinx after Ingres*, 1983.

22 An installation view of the David Hockney retrospective exhibition at the Tate Gallery from October 1988 to January 1989, showing, from left to right, *My Parents*, 1977, *Mr and Mrs Clark and Percy*, 1970–71, and *American Collectors*, 1968.

Norman Reid was able to strengthen considerably the holdings of abstract art, which did not appeal to his predecessor. When I arrived in 1980 it seemed important to get a better balanced collection by adding more Surrealist and Realist and Pop Art. The acquisition catalogues of the Tate are there to show what each of us has done. Directors of the Tate work closely with their Trustees and with their professional curatorial staff. I was particularly anxious that the voices of the younger curators should be heard, and was

always prepared to back their views when it came to purchasing work by artists under fifty. The very fact of a Tate purchase inevitably makes a great difference to the artist as he rises to fame.

No museum director has the power that rests with the active private collector. During my nine years at the Tate, I would sometimes think with envy of the way that Charles and Doris Saatchi were building up their remarkable private collection. Spending their own money, they could acquire exactly what they wanted. To be bought by the Saatchis was of considerable value to any artist. To be bought and then dropped was a heavy blow. But now we move into my third circle of recognition, the patronage of collectors and dealers.

23 Cézanne's portrait of the collector Victor Chocquet seated in an armchair, painted *c.* 1877–80. They had met in 1875, and Chocquet went on to acquire 35 works by Cézanne.

AS THE ARTIST ACHIEVES CRITICAL RECOGNITION, he is likely to find himself supported by collectors and dealers. Almost every major talent attracts one or two important collectors at an early stage in his career, and these collectors almost always appear on the scene because of their friendships with artists, whose advice they take. Sometimes these patrons have no record of collecting and begin because they are impressed by the personality of the artist rather than by his pictures. Eugène Murer, the collector of Renoir and Pissarro in the late 1870s, was a pastry cook who had been at school with Guillaumin and enjoyed the society of artists. Victor Chocquet was a modest customs official with a passion for Delacroix who met Renoir who in turn persuaded Chocquet to be one of the first to buy Cézanne's paintings.

It is the same with dealers. Those who promote the new and unfamiliar play a valuable and creative role. A young dealer is well advised to listen to his artist contemporaries, and find some major talent emerging to whom he can give his support. Daniel-Henry Kahnweiler is the classic example. He arrived in Paris in February 1907 aged twenty-two and immediately purchased the Fauve work of Matisse, Derain and Vlaminck. He used these purchases to win personal friendship with the artists he admired. He backed Braque and Picasso while they invented Cubism. Before he was thirty Kahnweiler had exclusive contracts with Picasso, Braque, Léger, Derain and Vlaminck. It is an extraordinary record, because Kahnweiler was at the same time encouraging the collectors of new art, such as Shchukin in Moscow and Rupf in Berne.

Even more important is the fact that Kahnweiler provided a gallery and exhibited the new paintings of his artists. This seems to me to be an innovation too little recognized. It marks a further and significant change in the way new art comes before the public. Until the later nineteenth century it was in the big annual exhibitions of the Royal Academy and the Paris Salon that the Pre-

24 The dealer Ambroise Vollard, portrayed by Renoir in 1908. He is presented as a connoisseur, examining a small sculpture by Maillol.

25 Vollard, painted less than two years later by Picasso, in 1909–10. The likeness is strong, despite the analytical cubist technique.

26 Picasso's portrait of the German-born dealer Daniel-Henry Kahnweiler, painted in 1910. The artist now takes considerable liberties with the appearance of his sitter, who is younger than himself.

Raphaelites or the Barbizon painters or Courbet or Manet first appeared. Then the independent exhibition societies take over: Sickert and the London Impressionists showed with the New English Art Club; the French Symbolists in the Indépendants; the Fauves in the Salon d'Automne. The inner circle of Cubists showed not in a big public forum, but at Kahnweiler's little gallery in the rue Vignon.

Kahnweiler was very loyal to his first loves: for him Picasso could never paint a poor picture. He was also remarkably blind to later developments in painting: none of his later protégés – Beaudin, Kermadec, Lascaux or Roger – made any mark.

Sometimes an established dealer looks for ways to continue in the modern art market, and if he has any sense he will ask his artists whom they admire. He may not get good advice, but if he does, and then acts upon it, he will be very successful. This is how Paul Durand-Ruel came to be the dealer of the Impressionists. The firm had made its name promoting Barbizon painting, and it was Daubigny who introduced Durand-Ruel to Monet in London in 1871, recommending that he buy his work. Durand-Ruel was already interested in the young Impressionists, and ready to give them substantial financial support.

Association with outstanding young artists helps a gallery to grow more quickly than any other way. Nicholas Logsdail's Lisson Gallery is a good example in London today, as was Kasmin's success with Hockney and others twenty-five years ago. Most of the leading art galleries in London have had a short phase when they were closely associated with the emergence of major new talents; the Lefevre showed Nicholson's abstract works in the 1930s and 1940s; Redfern supported English Neo-Romantics in the 1940s and 1950s; Gimpels backed such very unpopular abstract painters as Hilton and Lanyon and Davie in the 1950s, Waddington the other St Ives painters in the early 1960s, and so on.

27 Installation view of the Lisson Gallery, London, during the Richard Deacon exhibition, March 1987.

28 Installation view of Gimpel Fils Gallery, London, during the Summer exhibition of 1956. Work by Bernard Meadows, Ben Nicholson, Alan Davie, Peter Lanyon and others may be seen.

29 Installation view of the Saatchi Gallery, London, during the exhibition of Anselm
Kiefer paintings and Richard Serra sculptures, 1986–87.

One should also cite galleries that no longer exist, such as the Leicester, which backed Moore; the Hanover, which showed Bacon and Hamilton and Scott; Robert Fraser with Blake and Caulfield; or, perhaps the noblest of all, Mrs Lessore's Beaux Arts Gallery, which gave first exhibitions to Auerbach and Kossoff and so many others.

SO MUCH FOR MY THIRD CIRCLE OF RECOGNITION, that of the patrons, whether they be collectors or dealers. The final stage is the public acclaim that shows that the modern artist is truly famous. A contemporary example: the 1988 Hockney exhibition at the Tate Gallery, celebrating the artist's fiftieth birthday, was seen by 173,000 visitors. This broke the Tate record for a one-man retrospective exhibition by a living British artist, which had been held by Francis Bacon, with 110,000 visitors, for his 1985 exhibition. Bacon's career exactly follows the pattern I have outlined. Born in 1909, he began painting in 1928, largely self taught. Herbert Read illustrated his work in *Art Now*, published in 1933, but Bacon's first one-man exhibition in London was not held until 1949. There was one important collector, Robert Sainsbury. A first Tate retrospective that marked public recognition took place in 1962 when Bacon was fifty-two.

I think it takes about twenty-five years for the truly original artist to win public recognition. In the first ten years or so the work is too uncomfortable for it to be accepted, but slowly it wins through. In mid-career the artist can expect a change in public attitude. His work is now creating the taste by which it is enjoyed. This happened to Monet and Rodin with their exhibitions in 1900, when both men were sixty. When they died, aged eighty-six and seventy-seven respectively, they were universally respected and very rich. Artists who continue to work into old age leave great personal fortunes. Dali is said to have left £75 million; the works of art and investments held by the Henry Moore Foundation must be worth over £100 million. Picasso's estate was far in excess of these figures.

The corollary is that the artist must live into middle age to enjoy the benefits of this situation. If he dies young, for whatever reason, then the artistic career is likely to appear a failure, and myths about the unsuccessful artist begin to grow.

Let me instance the case of Van Gogh. He did not begin to paint until he was twenty-six, and his career lasted only eleven years. More than six of these were spent in the artistic backwater of the Netherlands: of the four years that remained, two were spent in Paris in what was in fact an apprenticeship to new painting. The first great paintings, done when Van Gogh moved to Arles early in 1888, were painted little more than two years before his death. Thus he simply did not live long enough to see success. Even so, Van Gogh had won recognition from his fellow artists, and the first major article, by Albert Aurier, had appeared in the *Mercure de France* in January 1890, six months before his suicide. The death of his beloved brother, Theo, certainly delayed public recognition for a decade, but from the Bernheim-Jeune exhibition in Paris in 1901 onwards his painting quickly won acceptance. Had Van Gogh lived to be eighty and died in 1933, he would certainly have been very famous and very rich.

The same is true of the other great Post-Impressionists. Seurat's life was cut short by illness at the age of thirty-two; Cézanne was slow to reach success, but this was partly the consequence of his own reluctance to show his work in Paris, and when the young dealer Vollard, following Pissarro's advice, showed a major exhibition of his work in 1895 all the art world recognized a master. The case of Gauguin is the most interesting one. For personal and artistic reasons he felt that he had to exile himself from Europe: had he remained in Paris I have no doubt that he too would have achieved considerable artistic and financial success.

I said that it takes about twenty-five years for the exceptional artist to win public recognition. But this is really true of all artists, whatever their ambitions. Some years ago I attempted a statistical analysis of the 1850 Royal Academy Summer Exhibition. At that moment in history there were no independent societies, or dealers' galleries, or museums exhibiting contemporary art in England, and the only way for a young artist to achieve recognition was to get his work into the Academy. This was the situation that confronted the young Pre-Raphaelites.

I had always lazily imagined that the Academy shows were full of work by old artists, and was surprised to discover that 70 per cent of the exhibitors were aged between twenty-five and forty. The great majority of the older exhibitors were Academicians or Associates: forty-three of these were showing paintings. They had normally been elected Associates in their early thirties, and could expect to be full Academicians by the time they were forty. In general, the Academicians tried to single out the outstanding new talents, regardless of style. Turner, already mentioned, is the exemplar. Constable was much slower to be accepted by the Academy, partly I believe because some thought him a rich amateur and not a true professional painter. When the Academicians gave up their open policy in the later nineteenth century, the Summer Exhibitions quickly lost their dominant position in British art.

To return to the 1850 exhibition, of the first 100 named artists, 14 are represented in the Tate Gallery collection today, but only 5 could be said to be remembered – Burton, Collins, Collinson, Cooper and Francis Danby – who is today the only well-known name, honoured with a Tate retrospective in 1989. So one in a hundred became famous. It is also clear that most artistic careers were very short. If artists did not succeed in getting elected to the Academy, they gave up and retired to teaching or administration or obscurity.

So far, I have been trying to describe the conditions of artistic success. I do not believe that there has been any major change in the way that this happens, ever since the artist won independence from the dominant patronage of Church, State or aristocrat in the eighteenth century. Such recent polemical concepts as the 'avant-garde' or 'Modernism' or 'feminism' do not seem to alter the position. It will have been evident from what I have been saying however that there are psychological and socio-economic factors that do play a great part in the way the modern artist rises to fame. They can interrupt the four-part process I have described, and may be constructive or destructive or merely benign. Both factors deserve some attention.

THE PSYCHOLOGY OF ARTISTIC CREATIVITY has not been much studied, and when it has been, the results have not been applied to art history. It is sometimes said that the creative personality is manic-depressive, and it is certainly true that many artists experience alternations of intense activity and fallow periods. This can impede progress. Then, on a more mundane level, there is the artist who makes a bad marriage, or takes to drink, or pursues a path of self-destruction. Such things happen in every walk of life, and art is not excluded.

There are two psychological phenomena more especially associated with the artist, however, which I find of considerable interest. The creative act is a unique and personal one, but it cannot exist in isolation. I do not believe that any great art has been produced in a non-competitive situation: on the contrary it is the fiercely competitive environment in which the young artist finds himself that drives him to excel. He has to make an enormous effort to lift himself above his contemporaries. This results in what we often call the 'breakthrough', that every artist on the path to success has to make.

Having achieved this, the artist generally continues to work at a high level of creativity for a number of years, and then, for one reason or another, he begins to fade a little. This is what I propose calling the phenomenon of 'ten (or even five) good years'. In many cases, artists never quite recover the quality of their early breakthrough period: in some cases their work declines markedly. This phenomenon is not new: with certain qualifications, I would say that it is true of Delacroix, from the *Massacre of Chios* (1824) to the *Women of Algiers* (1834) or even only to the *Death of Sardanapalus* (1827–28); of Courbet, from the *Burial at Ornans* (1849) to the *Atelier* (1855); of Holman Hunt and John Everett Millais between 1849 and 1855; of Duchamp, from the *Nude Descending* to the *Large Glass*; of Chirico, from 1911 to 1917; and so on. Many artists do their best work in a relatively short period.

Having made the breakthrough and had his five or ten good years the real problem that confronts the artist is to sustain a career. There are inevitably going to be periods of neglect and rejection, particularly when a younger generation with very different ideas appears on the scene. Mid-career art often has a particular feel about it, as of course does 'late work'. There is, it seems, a graph of creativity which can be plotted through an artist's career.

I have said that artistic creativity is competitive, and my second phenomenon also relates to this. Most truly original new art is the result of group activity. It appears that the conjunction of several exceptional talents results in something that is greater than the parts. The history of new developments in painting and sculpture is largely a chain formed of pairs and trios and larger groupings. Turner and Girtin, Delacroix and Géricault, the Pre-Raphaelites, Barbizon painters, Fauves, Cubists, Brücke and Blaue Reiter – one can continue. The great artists who emerge from such group-based developments are completely individual of course, but at an early stage they seem to need this communal support.

30 Photograph of artists and critics at the First International Surrealist
Exhibition, held in London in June 1936. Among those standing are

Salvador Dali, Paul Eluard, Roland Penrose, Herbert Read; Eileen
Agar is seated centre.

The originality of John Rewald's great book *The History of Impressionism* lay in his detailed description of a network of close personal relationships, out of which four of the greatest painters of all time emerged, Manet and Degas, Cézanne and Monet. The more modestly talented artists in the circle – Renoir, Pissarro, Sisley – were stimulated to produce art of a very high quality. A second, Post-Impressionist, generation – Gauguin, Seurat and Van Gogh – equalled the achievement of the first. Rewald's book was published in New York in 1946, and the story of American Abstract Expressionist painting in the 1940s and early 1950s was remarkably similar. Pollock, Rothko, Newman, Still and de Kooning were all linked together in friendship and rivalry. A Post-Expressionist generation of distinction – Johns, Lichtenstein, Rauschenberg, Warhol – was to follow them. Artists who emerge from such a situation do not have a consistency of style – indeed, they tend to move to extremes – but there is a consistency of purpose. They want to get to the top.

IT IS BECAUSE OF THIS that what I have called relocation is necessary. At certain moments in the history of art (not at all times) one place assumes a dominant position. In the nineteenth century, once the challenge from London collapsed under Victorian complacency, Paris won this position with Corot, Courbet and Manet, and confirmed it with the Impressionist and Post-Impressionist generations. Van Gogh had to come to Paris; so did the Norwegian Munch. The twenty-five-year-old Munch arrived in Paris in 1889 and stayed for three years, making contact with Gauguin and the Symbolists. This visit was crucial to Munch's painting. His best work is concentrated on the years 1892–95, when he was leading a peripatetic existence, staying in Berlin as well as Paris. Munch is an excellent example of an artist with 'five good years'.

31 R.B. Kitaj's painting of *The Jew, Etc.*, 1976–79.

In the first part of the twentieth century, the burgeoning process of relocation in Paris transformed French art into international art. Of particular importance was the Jewish contribution, of a richness and variety out of proportion to numbers, as if a great flood of creativity had suddenly been released. Chagall, Lipchitz, Soutine, Modigliani and Epstein all arrived in Paris shortly after 1900, meeting Spaniards, Germans, Italians, Romanians. Perhaps the Jewish artists found it easiest to relocate; the idea of the artist as a natural wanderer, even outcast, has a strong pull on the Jewish imagination, as we see from the current preoccupations of R. B. Kitaj.

But what happened to French art? It seemed to collapse under the weight of internationalism, so that since Dubuffet's death there has been no French painter or sculptor of the first rank, apart from the aging Balthus. In so far as there was a capital for art from the 1940s onwards it was New York, and though New York may still claim the title, the critical consensus today is that New York is in decline. I believe that the creative centre has already moved back to Europe, though no longer situated in any one place. There is no need for an artist to move to New York to get to the top: Anselm Kiefer's rapid (and deserved) rise to fame in the United States confirms this.

RELOCATION IS A MATTER OF ARTISTIC CHOICE: dislocation a matter of necessity. Mondrian's relocation in Paris in 1912 was a deliberate decision, so was his move to London in 1938: his final move to New York in 1940 was a consequence of war. Thus we reach the group of political and socio-economic conditions which affect the way the artist achieves success.

The two World Wars and the dictatorships of Hitler and Stalin had an enormously damaging effect on twentieth-century art, much greater, I believe, than is generally recognized. It is not only a question of talent, or potential talent, killed in the wars or destroyed in the camps. Too many artistic careers were disrupted by war or by emigration: the natural development of a creative artist was interrupted and permanently damaged.

The Second World War was a total war of a kind unknown in the nineteenth century. A younger generation of artists was altogether unable to practise their art. When Victor Pasmore and Michael Tippett insisted on doing so, refusing to participate in the war, they were sent to prison. Older artists had to move. Lipchitz, Léger, Ernst, Miró, Dali and many others left Paris for New York, and this partly explains why the world's artistic capital moved across the Atlantic in the 1940s. Another reason is that the generation of de Kooning and Pollock would have been conscripted for military service had they been Europeans.

American hospitality was generous, and the cultural benefits of the emigration, particularly Jewish emigration, were very consider-able. Britain was also fortunate, as we are reminded by the contribution of such now assimilated painters as the Berlin-born Freud and Auerbach, or indeed of the great publishing house whose founder this essay celebrates. But this should not blind us to the fact that in the case of certain artists the consequences of dislocation were disastrous. This is very clearly seen if one turns for a moment to music. In my opinion Schoenberg composed nothing of real consequence in almost twenty years in the United States, and Bartok's American work, including the popular *Concerto for Orchestra*, shows a sad decline. Britten's decision to return to England in 1942 perhaps saved his career, and resulted in a succession of masterpieces from *Peter Grimes* onwards. There is an interesting comparison to be made between the universally successful *War Requiem* (1961) and the very similarly intentioned but now forgotten requiem, *When lilacs bloomed*, by Paul Hinde-mith (1946), who had settled in the United States in 1940.

I must also confess that I find it hard to see Mondrian's final

57

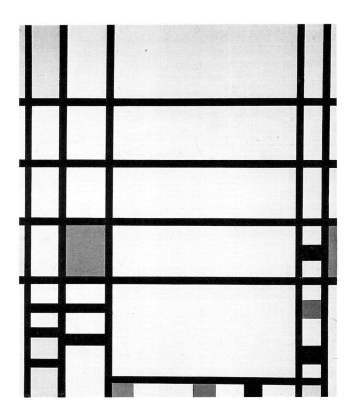

32 *(left)* Mondrian's *Trafalgar Square*, 1939–43, conceived during his two-year stay in London, 1938–40, and completed in New York.

33 *(right)* Mondrian's *Broadway Boogie-Woogie* of 1942–43, one of the last pictures, painted in New York shortly before the artist's death in 1944.

New York paintings as the culmination of his career, which is the accepted opinion, certainly in the United States. They seem to me completely unresolved and uncertain in handling, altogether lacking that serene harmony of composition that Mondrian had achieved in Europe between the wars. It was the troubled times in which he lived that prevented Mondrian realizing even a modest financial success. Yet by 1986, forty-two years after his death in New York at the age of seventy-two, an oil painting of 1938 was sold for $5 million. You could have bought it from Mondrian in London in 1939 for £50. Some people did acquire his paintings at this time: the artists Barbara Hepworth and Ben Nicholson, the writer Nicolette Gray, one or two private collectors who were their

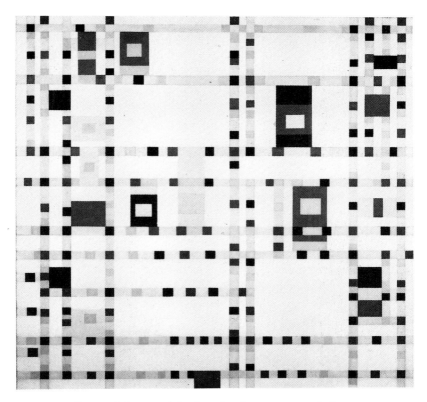

friends. Recognition of Mondrian at this time had not proceeded very far; by my scale he was still in the second circle.

Today, because of the relatively settled nature of the economy since the end of the Second World War, this situation simply would not happen. Money men have moved into the art market, intent on exploiting the exceptional talents. Do the artists benefit? Jasper Johns and Francis Bacon see their new paintings sold for $1 million and more: there must be a dozen British artists whose top prices are now over £100,000. This financial success is all of course quite irrelevant to the quality of the work, and can even be inhibiting to the artist. One might also wish that some of this money were available to the exceptional artist at an earlier stage in his or her career. It should never be forgotten that a high proportion of the artists of genius in the nineteenth century benefitted from a private income – Delacroix, Courbet, Manet, Degas, Cézanne were all *rentiers* – and this gave them a certain freedom to pursue their own ideas that artists from a less financially secure background – Renoir, or Monet, for example – simply did not have. Indeed, one could argue that the intransigence of a Cézanne was only possible in such circumstances.

As such private incomes are things of the past, it becomes vital to ensure that small sums are available from the State to nurture the outstanding talents. The fact that there are so many outstanding painters and sculptors in their forties and fifties in the United Kingdom is partly a consequence of enlightened state patronage twenty years or so ago. If this is absent, and everything is left to the workings of the market, the world of art will in due course be much the poorer.

We now see modern art exploited for political as well as economic reasons. It is generally agreed that in the 1950s and 1960s the American Government actively promoted the Abstract Expressionist artists who emerged in New York in the 1940s. There was a useful analogy between the freedom and expansiveness of the painting and the image of the United States which was being presented worldwide. Such cultural politics can falsify a situation, leading to the over-valuation of one group of artists at the expense of another. There seems to be an expectation at the moment that interesting painting is coming out of Gorbachov's Russia. In my opinion this is journeyman art – of no great consequence. Stalin destroyed the great visual art of Russia, and it will take a decade or more before any major painter or sculptor appears. Interestingly, in music the situation is quite different, and there are half a dozen Soviet composers of real potential. The reason for this is simple: Stalin could not destroy Shostakovich, so that Soviet musical standards remained high when artistic standards collapsed. American postwar music has in comparison always remained provincial, by contrast to the visual arts – the one major figure, Elliot Carter, has been consistently neglected in the United States and left on one side in order to promote the maverick John Cage, and now the much more approachable but probably ephemeral minimalist composers.

In his travel book *Beyond the Mexique Bay*, published in 1934, Aldous Huxley wrote: 'The truth is, of course, that most art has always been either bad or indifferent. This is inevitable. Artistic talent is an extremely rare phenomenon.' Huxley went on to say that the only substitute for personal talent is a good artistic tradition, which he defined as: 'the ghosts of good dead artists dictating to bad living artists'. But this begs a lot of questions which it would take another essay to discuss.

I do not however dissent from Huxley's judgment: good art is extremely uncommon. One can pretend not to recognize it, and treat all art as being of equal validity, any choice being a matter of personal taste. But as will have been made clear I do not accept this position: there is a selecting process inexorably at work, and those of us who spend time buying and exhibiting contemporary art, writing and talking about it, even simply looking at it, are playing a part in that process. Art, like science, is highly selective.

Artists have to strive for recognition at the early stages of their careers, knowing that their chances of success are small. But the exceptional talents will always be recognized, usually from a very early stage, and their paths to fame will follow the pattern of progress that I have indicated. To imagine that there are unrecognized geniuses working away in isolation somewhere, waiting to be discovered, is simply not credible. Great art doesn't happen like that.

LIST OF ILLUSTRATIONS

Measurements are given in centimetres, followed by inches in brackets.

Height precedes width.

1 The author with Alison Smithson at the *54:64 Painting and Sculpture of a Decade* exhibition at the Tate Gallery, London, 22 April – 28 June 1964
Photo courtesy Tate Gallery Archives, London

2 J. M. W. TURNER (1775–1851)
Transept of Ewenny Priory, Glamorganshire, Exh. RA 1797
Watercolour, 40 × 56.5 ($15\frac{3}{4}$ × $22\frac{1}{4}$)
National Museum of Wales, Cardiff

3 VINCENT VAN GOGH (1853–90)
Irises, 1889
Oil on canvas, 73 × 93 ($28\frac{3}{4}$ × $36\frac{5}{8}$)
Private Collection

4 DAVID HOCKNEY (b.1937)
November, 1959
Oil, size unknown
Photo courtesy of the artist

5 DAVID HOCKNEY (b.1937)
We Two Boys Together Clinging, 1961
Oil on board, 122 × 153 (48 × 60)
Arts Council Collection, South Bank Centre, London

6 R. B. KITAJ (b.1932)
The Red Banquet, 1960
Oil and collage on canvas, 122 × 122 (48 × 48)
Walker Art Gallery, Liverpool

7 ALLEN JONES (b.1937)
The Battle of Hastings, 1961–2
Oil on canvas, 182.9 × 182.9 (72 × 72)
Tate Gallery, London

8 DANTE GABRIEL ROSSETTI (1828–82)
Self-portrait, 1855
Pen and ink, 16 × 14.2 ($6\frac{1}{4}$ × $5\frac{5}{8}$)
William Morris Gallery, Walthamstow

9 WILLIAM HOLMAN HUNT (1827–1910)
John Everett Millais, 1853
Pastel and chalk, 32.7 × 24.8 ($12\frac{7}{8}$ × $9\frac{3}{4}$)
National Portrait Gallery, London

10 WILLIAM HOLMAN HUNT (1827–1910)
Self-portrait, 1845
Oil on canvas, 45.7 × 39.4 (18 × $15\frac{1}{2}$)
City Museum and Art Gallery, Birmingham

11 HENRI FANTIN-LATOUR (1836–1904)
L'Atelier des Batignolles, 1870
Oil on canvas, 174 × 208.3 ($68\frac{1}{2}$ × 82)
Louvre, Paris
Photo Bulloz

12 MAX PECHSTEIN (1881–1955)
Poster for *Die Brücke* Exhibition at Galerie Emil Richter, Dresden, 1909
Woodcut illustration

13 EDOUARD MANET (1832–83)
Emile Zola, 1867–8
Oil on canvas, 146 × 114.3 ($57\frac{1}{2}$ × 45)
Musée d'Orsay, Paris
Photo Giraudon

14 GUSTAVE COURBET (1819–77)
Portrait of Baudelaire, c. 1848
Oil on canvas, 53 × 61 ($20\frac{7}{8}$ × 24)
Musée Fabre, Montpellier
Photo Bulloz

15 C. W. COPE (1811–90)
*The Council of the Royal Academy Selecting
   Pictures for the Exhibition*, 1876
Oil on canvas, 144.8 × 219.7 (57 × $86\frac{1}{2}$)
Royal Academy, London

16 The first-floor gallery of the Paris Salon
   in 1852
Photograph by Gustave Le Gray
Collection André Jammes

17 Poster for the Fifth Impressionist
   Exhibition, Paris, 1880

18 ROGER FRY (1866–1934)
*View of the Second Post-Impressionist
   Exhibition*, 1912
Oil on wood, 50.8 × 61 (20 × 24)
Musée d'Orsay, Paris
Photo Réunion des musées nationaux

19 Photograph of one of the Van Gogh
   rooms at the Sonderbund Exhibition in
   Cologne, 1912

20 Installation view of *54:64 Painting and
   Sculpture of a Decade* exhibition at the
   Tate Gallery, London, 22 April –
   28 June 1964
Photo courtesy Tate Gallery Archives,
London

21 Installation view of Francis Bacon
   retrospective, Tate Gallery, London,
   22 May – 18 August 1985
Photo courtesy Tate Gallery Archives,
London

22 Installation view of David Hockney
   retrospective, Tate Gallery, London,
   26 October 1988 – 8 January 1989
Photo courtesy Tate Gallery Archives,
London

23 PAUL CÉZANNE (1839–1906)
Victor Chocquet in an Armchair, c. 1877
Oil on canvas, 45.1 × 36.8 ($17\frac{3}{4}$ × $14\frac{1}{2}$)
Columbus Museum of Art, Ohio;
   Museum Purchase, Howald Fund

24 AUGUSTE RENOIR (1841–1919)
Ambroise Vollard, 1908
Oil on canvas, 81.6 × 65.2 ($32\frac{1}{8}$ × $25\frac{5}{8}$)
Courtauld Institute Galleries,
   London (Courtauld Collection)

25 PABLO PICASSO (1881–1973)
Portrait of Ambroise Vollard, 1910
Oil on canvas, 92 × 64.9 ($36\frac{1}{4}$ × $25\frac{1}{2}$)
Pushkin Museum, Moscow
Photo Giraudon

26 PABLO PICASSO (1881–1973)
Daniel Henry Kahnweiler, 1910
Oil on canvas, 100.5 × 72.6 ($39\frac{5}{8}$ × $28\frac{5}{8}$)
Courtesy of the Art Institute of Chicago

27 Installation view of Richard Deacon
   Exhibition at the Lisson Gallery,
   London, March 1987
Photo Gareth Winters
Courtesy Lisson Gallery, London

28 Installation view of Gimpel Fils
   Summer Exhibition, London, 1956
Photo Gimpel Fils, London

29 Installation view of Anselm Kiefer and
   Richard Serra Exhibition at the Saatchi
   Collection, London, September 1986 –
   July 1987
Photo Jenny Okun
Courtesy Saatchi Collection, London

30 Artists and writers at the First
   International Surrealist Exhibition,
   London, 1936
Photo courtesy Eileen Agar

31 R. B. KITAJ (b.1932)
The Jew, Etc., 1976–9
Oil and charcoal on canvas, 152.4 × 121.9
   (60 × 48)
Marlborough Fine Art (London) Ltd

32 PIET MONDRIAN (1872–1944)
Trafalgar Square, 1939–43
Oil on canvas, 149 × 119 ($58\frac{5}{8} \times 46\frac{7}{8}$)
Private Collection, New York
Photo courtesy Sidney Janis Gallery, New
   York

33 PIET MONDRIAN (1872–1944)
Broadway Boogie-Woogie, 1942–43
Oil on canvas, 127 × 127 (50 × 50)
Collection the Museum of Modern Art,
   New York